The Best Option Strategies:

A "Hands On" Guide to Making Money with Options

Volume 1

Writing Naked Puts

Mark D Wolfinger

Writing Naked Puts

Mark D Wolfinger

This is Book TWO in a series of educational and informative books for option traders.

Volume 0: Introduction to Options: The Basics
Volume 1: Writing Naked Puts
Volume 2: Iron Condors

Requests to the publisher should be addressed to
Mark D Wolfinger; 1717 Dobson Street; Evanston, IL 60202

The Purpose of this Series of Books

These e-books are not for the options novice (exception: Volume 0). They are intended for investors and traders who already understand how options work and who want to put that knowledge to work to make money.

Each volume contains a thorough discussion of one specific option strategy or topic. None of the topics covered in the series is a high-risk gamble. I offer no get rich quick schemes, nor outrageous promises of enormous profits. These books represent the 'nuts and bolts' (basics for the non-novice) of strategies that work.

Rather than trade a single option strategy, it is efficient to have a strategy arsenal and choose something appropriate for current market conditions. Writing naked puts is one such strategy.

These books are aimed at two target audiences:

- The reader who lacks experience using the specific strategy.

- A quick, but thorough tutorial is provided

- The reader who already understands the basics of the strategy and who wants a more thorough understanding of

    o How the strategy makes money

    o When and why one uses the strategy

    o How to manage risk when using the strategy

This book is not (yet) for readers who are encountering options for the first. Begin your basic options education by reading: The Rookie's Guide to Options, 2nd edition, 2013 by Mark D Wolfinger.

This is VOLUME 1: Writing Naked Put Options

None of the terms used in this book should be unfamiliar, but a glossary (terms underlined and in bold) is available, if needed.

Table of Contents

Introduction

Selling naked put options is often (mistakenly) considered to be a 'very risky' proposition. Professional stockbrokers who spread that message are doing their customers a major disservice, because they are steering those customers away from a prudent, profitable investment method.

The only dangerous part of options trading is the risk-insensitive trader who buys and sells options with little or no understanding of just what can go wrong. The options, by themselves, are not dangerous tools.

I mention that because one of the long-lasting misconceptions about options is that they are dangerous to use. The truth: It is possible to use options to speculate (gamble), but options were created as hedging, or risk-reducing, investment tools. An alarming number of financial professionals, including stockbrokers, financial planners and journalists are in position to educate the public about the many advantages to be gained from adopting naked put writing (and other option strategies), but fail to do so. Many public investors never bother to make an effort to learn about options once they hear negative statements from professional advisors.

Except for extremely bearish prognosticators, no one ever suggests that owning stock is anything but the most prudent of investment strategies. It is certainly recommended as a viable long-term strategy for "widows and orphans." The idea of writing naked put options is significantly more conservative and definitely less risky than simply buying and owning stocks – yet it remains invisible to investors who rely on professionals for advice. Selling put options deserves to be considered as an attractive investment alternative for millions of investors.

1

Mark D Wolfinger

Readers of this e-book are probably already aware of the benefits that come with writing (selling) put options. Join me as I explain some of the finer points of this strategy including how to manage risk.

How to Use this Book

This is a hands-on guide to making money with options.

Part I Discussion

Part I contains background information that provides a better understanding of why writing put options is an attractive strategy for anyone with a bullish market bias. NOTE: Selling naked puts involves downside risk —the same risk associated with owning stock. However, put sellers lose less money when markets decline.

One pitfall is that profits are limited and the very, very bullish trader should probably find a different strategy. Remember that bull markets come and go, but put writing is worth learning because it is an intelligent choice when markets are neutral to mildly bullish.

This strategy is especially attractive to you, the investor who accumulates stock over time, because it allows the purchase of stock at attractive prices. And if it turns out that you fail to get your stock at that favorable price, then you receive a cash consolation prize (the option premium). Think of it from the standpoint of a typical investor who enters a below-market bid for the stock and never buys the stock. The put writer won't buy the stock either, but he earns a profit when the put option is repurchased or expires worthless.

Writing naked put options appeals to you, *the trader*, because it provides a higher probability of earning a profit from the trade compared with buying stock. It also offers the possibility of making money from a bullish position, even when the stock price declines (by a small amount). It is heartwarming to earn that profit when your predictive powers failed. That situation is unknown to the bullish trader whose arsenal of strategies only allows for making money when the market rises.

Part I begins with a discussion of who can benefit and why they may want to adopt this strategy. Part I covers writing naked put options from both a theoretical and practical point of view.

Part II. The Nuts and Bolts

Part II covers trading ideas: how to think about a trade, how to prepare for a trade, how to enter and exit the trade, how to repair a trade (manage risk) – if and when it becomes necessary, and how to prepare for expiration (the day the options expire).

Part I Background and Discussion

1. Who should consider writing naked puts?

2. Strategy Objective

2. Strategy description

4. Profit Potential. Why this Strategy Works

5. Risk Considerations

6. Margin

7. Trading Expenses

8. Using Calculators to Determine Option Theoretical Values

Chapter 1

Who Should Write Naked (Uncovered) Puts?

Naked put writing is not for everyone. However, the majority of people who buy stock for an investment portfolio can benefit from this strategy. If you are someone who does not pick individual stocks, then you may prefer to sell puts on exchange traded funds (ETFs) or market indexes.

I recommend naked put selling for:

Investors

- Who are bullish on the market.
- Who are bullish on specific stocks.
- Who want to buy a specific stock at a lower price.
- Who adopt a buy and hold strategy.
- Who want additional income from their holdings.

Traders

- Who want a higher percentage of winning trades.
- Willing to consider holding a position for a month or two.
- Who want to begin a spread position with a bullish leg.

Chapter 2
Strategy Objective

Why would you want to write naked puts? What is there to be gained?

Writing puts is a bullish strategy. When selling the put, there are two possible investment objectives:

Earn a trading profit. You are bullish on the stock and expect the put option to lose value, and perhaps expire worthless. The option premium (minus the cost of closing the trade becomes the profit.

Buy stock at a discount. If the put option is in the money when expiration arrives, you will be assigned an exercise notice and be obligated to buy the stock you want to own at a discount to today's price. This is an intelligent method for an investor to gradually add positions to a long-term portfolio. **NOTE:** When you are eventually assigned that exercise notice, the stock will be below your target purchase price. However, if you had entered an order to buy stock at your target price, you would be in worse shape than the put seller (whose loss is cushioned by the premium collected).

Example
WXY is trading @ $30 and you are willing to buy shares @ $27 or less. You can accomplish this goal by writing a put option with a 30-strike price, when the premium is $3 or more.

Here is how it works: You collect $3 per share now by selling the put. If assigned later, you pay $30 per share. Thus, the net cost is $27 per share. If, for example, the stock never trades below $29, then you own shares $2 below the lowest real-market price. Now that is a bargain!

7

The option seller receives cash (the premium). That cash is yours to keep, no matter what else happens. In return for that cash, you accept certain obligations - specifically you give the put owner the right to force you to buy 100 shares of the specific stock at the **strike price** for a limited time. You have no say as to whether you are eventually forced to buy the stock. That decision, and the timing of that decision, rests entirely with the option owner.

When you write (sell) put options, and continue to hold the position through the option expiration date, there are only two possible outcomes, depending on the price of the underlying stock. Each of the possible outcomes is a win for you, the investor. Either you buy stock at your price, or you keep the premium as the profit.

If you are a trader with a short-term objective, then you are likely to have a better result from selling puts than if you bought the stock. However, every so often the stock soars and the put seller is left holding only a small profit.

Expiration results

If the put finishes (based on the stock price at the close of business on expiration Friday) in the money, you are assigned an exercise notice and must buy 100 shares of stock (a stock you want to own) at a steep discount to its price when you originated the trade

- The net cost of the stock is the strike price of the option, less the cash premium received when selling the put option

- If the put finishes **out of the money**, it expires worthless. You don't buy stock, but earn a quick profit (the premium) instead

TIP: It is often a wise move (and always a good risk-management move) to repurchase the short option when it becomes available at a very low price (perhaps $0.05 or $0.10). I suggest taking this conservative action whenever there is at least one week remaining before expiration. More conservative investors should consider buying the option for $.05 or $.10 as standard operating procedure — even when less time remains. This action frees your capital for other investments and avoids the unhappy mess in which you lose hundreds or even thousands of dollars trying to earn an extra $5 or $10 per option.

Mark D Wolfinger

Chapter 3
Strategy Description

NOTE: Naked put writing is equivalent in risk and profit potential to the strategy known as covered call writing. In fact, a covered call position is often called a synthetic put.

NOTE: No proof is offered here because readers of this book should already be familiar with this concept. If not, take a look at The Rookie's Guide to Options, 2nd edition, or read my July 2008 blog post (see Appendix) on equivalent positions.

To begin, certain decisions must be made: First choose the underlying stock, based on one of these criteria:

- A stock you are willing (or eager) to own.

- A price you are willing to pay.

- A stock whose price you believe will not decline (below the put strike price) over the lifetime of the option.

> **NOTE: This is the heart and soul of the strategy and the reason that it is so attractive:**
>
> **Profitable trades are more common because it is much easier to find a stock that does not decline below the put strike price than it is to find a stock that will rally.**

Let me repeat that: It is easier to find a stock whose price will not decline than it is to find a stock whose price will increase. In traditional investing, the only path to profits is to buy something that increases in value. When writing naked put options, you also make money when the stock price increases. However, there is also a nice profit when the stock price holds steady or even when it declines – as long as the decline is small.

If a stock is trading near $32 per share, you will earn money more often if you bet that it will not move below $30 per share (by selling puts with a $30 strike price) than if you bet it will move higher (by buying shares). If it is not obvious why this is true, recognize that every time the price is above $32 and the stock buyer earns a profit, the stock is also above $30 and the put seller earns a profit. However, when the stock is priced between $30 and $32 on the option expiration date, the put seller gains and the stock buyer loses.

This is not a strategy adopted by everyone because traditional investors can earn unlimited profits — and that is a very attractive possibility. Put sellers never earn more than the premium collected, and thus profits are limited. If you want to go for the jackpot, then writing puts is not for you. On the other hand, if you want better odds of success and if you are willing to accept limited (but decent) profits, writing puts is a strategy worthy of your consideration.

Next: decide which put option to write

Choose the premium

- The premium represents the maximum possible profit, so do not settle for too little.

- The higher the premium, the greater your risk of losing money, so do not be too greedy

Choose the put strike price

- Choose a strike that offers a good compromise for your expectations. The higher premium is good, but options with a smaller chance of moving into the money are also good.

NOTE: Do not plan on holding the position until the option expires. If the stock price declines and approaches the strike, it will probably be a wise idea to take defensive action (i.e., manage risk) and exit with a loss. If the stock price rises, consider leaving the last few pennies on the table and exiting early.

How much risk are you willing to take?

- The farther out of the money (OTM) the strike price, the more likely it is that the put will expire worthless.

- The farther OTM, the less premium can be collected.

How badly do you want to buy stock?

- If you want to own stock, choose an option that is not far OTM. This is something an investor may try.

- If you prefer to earn a trading profit and are not anxious to own stock, choose an option that is farther OTM. This is how a trader (as compared with an investor) thinks.

Choose the put expiration date

- How long do you want to own the position? Remember that your capital is tied up until the position is closed.

- Options with less time to expiration give the seller

- o Lower premium and less potential profit per trade.

- o A greater annualized return on investment (you can make more trades each year).

- o More negative gamma (i.e., losses accelerate more quickly).

TIP: Choose an expiration date that offers a profit potential (after expenses) that meets your objectives in both total dollars earned and annualized return.

There is no 'best' put to choose because each investor/trader has a different investment objective and a different risk tolerance. If you are uncertain how much profit is 'enough', you will gain confidence in your ability to make this decision as you gain experience. For readers who are new to using this strategy, avoid selling low-priced options. For example, never sell options at $0.05 or $0.10. NOTE: A low-priced option cannot be defined in dollar terms because so much of the option premium is defined by the stock price (higher priced stocks have options with a higher premium) and its volatility (more volatile stocks have options with a higher premium), and sometimes a $1 premium qualifies as 'small.'

Chapter 4
Profit Potential: What You Have to Gain

The maximum profit occurs when the put expires worthless. However, the longer the position is held, the greater the chances of seeing the put increase in value because of a stock price decline. NOTE: I assume all readers understand options well enough to know that put sellers can lose money when stock prices decline.

My suggested compromise is to exit all trades prior to expiration based on these two factors

- Have you earned enough profit to be satisfied?

- Is there enough remaining potential profit to hold longer? Let someone else earn the last nickel or two on the trade.

Commissions play an important role in determining your long-term trading profits. When the put expires worthless, there are no additional commissions. If you are assigned an exercise notice on any option, most brokers (but not all) charge a fee. Be sure that you know how much your broker charges for exercise and assignment.

IMPORTANT TIP: *Saving money on trading expenses is a good idea. However, risk management comes first and it is a poor idea to hold onto a position for the sole purpose of saving money on commissions. When risk is out of line with the possible reward, make an adjustment, or exit the trade.*

The Numbers
Profits and losses can be calculated in different ways, so choose a method that makes sense to you. Remember that the holding period is significant in determining the ROI (return

on an investment), so annualize the theoretical profit when comparing puts that expire on different dates.

When selling naked puts in a retirement account you are required to be cash backed, i.e., there must be sufficient cash in your account to pay for the stock, just in case you are assigned an exercise notice on the put options.

Example:

You write 5 puts struck at (that means the strike price is) 20, receiving $200 for each put. To pay for 500 shares @ $20 your account must have $10,000 cash to make this trade. You may use the proceeds from the put sale. Thus, you must have $9,000 cash ($10,000 less the $1,000 premium.)

The maximum possible profit is $1,000; on the $9,000 investment. Thus, the maximum ROI is 11.1%. If this is a one-month trade, then the annualized ROI is 11.1 *12, or 133%.

If you use the leverage available from a margin account, your potential profit (as a percentage) is greater (but so is the sum that can be lost).

Example:

If the margin requirement for this trade is $3,000, then your potential profit is $1,000 on a $3,000 investment, or 33.3% (or, assuming a one-month trade, 400% annualized).

Chapter 5

Risk Considerations

To minimize risk of a disaster, sell only "cash-backed" puts. If there is always enough cash to buy stock (if assigned) you will never receive a margin call (forcing you to deposit cash or liquidate the position).

Money will be lost when the prices of your stocks decline, but by not trading on margin, your account will never be wiped out. Don't think that it cannot happen. However, if you are never exposed to the possibility of a gigantic and sudden loss, then you will never have to face such a loss.

IRA accounts have strict risk limits. Many brokers allow naked put selling in IRA accounts, but only if the puts are cash-backed. If your broker does not allow the sale of cash secured puts in a retirement account, I strongly suggest that you find another broker.

Naked put writing allows stock to be accumulated at a discount, but that does not protect you from loss. The risk (bear market) of owning stock must be considered when adopting this strategy.

Using leverage allows a greater percentage return on your investment, but there are risks:

- You may be forced to liquidate the position at an inconvenient time.

- You can lose more money than when the position is not leveraged.

Mark D Wolfinger

Chapter 6

Margin Requirements

When writing naked puts, and electing to use margin (i.e., borrowing money from your broker rather than being cash backed, you must have collateral in your account. Your broker's requirement may be stricter, but this is the minimum margin requirement:

The initial margin requirement is ($250 minimum):

> 20% of the price of the underlying stock plus

> The premium collected from the option sale minus

> The amount that the put option is out of the money

TIP: Margin is less (15% vs. 20%) when selling puts on certain broad-based indexes.

Example

Stock is $28

Sell 10 Nov 25 puts @ $1.00

Options are out of the money by 3 points, or $300

Margin requirement for selling 10 puts is:

20% of stock price = 28 * 1000 * 0.20 = $5,600

Premium collected = 10 * 100 = $1,000

Out of money amount = 300 * 10 = $3,000

Margin requirement = $5,600 + $1,000 − $3,000 = $3,600

(or $360 for each put sold).

Mark D Wolfinger

Chapter 7

Trading Expenses

This strategy involves frequent trading and commissions matter. Consider using a deep discount broker (if you are not already doing so). Trade online to further reduce commissions.

Assignment fees can be higher than the commissions to trade stock, and must be taken into consideration in your calculations. Be aware of all possible expenses charged by your broker.

TIP: There is at least one online broker (InteractiveBrokers) who does not charge anything for an assignment notice, so do your homework.

NOTE: If you are trading only one or two option contracts per trade, commissions are especially important when your broker has a 'per ticket' charge.

Example:

If you write one put option @ $0.55, you collect $55.

The maximum possible profit is $55.

If the cost to execute a trade is $15, that represents more than 30% of the total option premium.

If you are eventually assigned an exercise notice and must pay a $20 fee, then your option sale netted only $20. Please be alert to costs if you are a small trader.

Possible solutions:

a) Find a less expensive broker (The best solution).

b) Trade one or two additional contracts per trade – but do not increase risk beyond the borders of your comfort zone.

c) Write options with high premiums (perhaps $150).

There is one other important consideration. Saving money on commissions is not the only item of importance. Some brokers are much better at executing trades. If you choose an inexpensive broker just to save on commissions, it is possible to lose an extra $5 or $10 on every option traded. This is much more costly than worrying about commissions.

NOTE: If you lose $0.05 by getting a poor fill from your broker on a 10-lot trade, that is $50.

NOTE: Some brokers have fewer restrictions and allow a greater variety of option strategies. If that's important to you, it may be worth paying higher commissions to gain access to those strategies.

In short, there is more to consider than just commission costs when choosing a broker – but it is difficult to make good money writing naked put options if your brokerage costs are high.

Chapter 8
Using Calculators

At approximately the same time that options began trading on an exchange (April 1973; the Chicago Board Options Exchange listed call options on 16 different stocks and the investment world has never been the same.), Fisher Black, Myron Scholes and Robert Merton developed a formula for calculating the theoretical value (and other properties of) stock options. This work produced the Black-Scholes Option Pricing Model that is still widely used (with modifications) today. The importance work was recognized with the Nobel Prize in Economics in 1997. Sadly this recognition occurred after the death of Fisher Black.

Today option-pricing calculators are readily available. All brokers provide calculators for customers, but if you want something different use an Internet search engine.

Reasons for using a calculator:

- To determine the fair value of an option.

- You will make more money over the long run, if you avoid writing options for less than their fair value.

- To determine the probability that an option will be in the money when expiration arrives, the option's Delta represents that probability.

- To determine the probability an option will expire worthless (It is 100 minus Delta.)

Calculators are most often used to determine the fair, or theoretical, value of an option. It is beyond the scope of this book to enter into a discussion on this topic, but be aware that the value of any option is based on the following factors:

Stock price

Type of option (put or call)

Strike price

Number of days remaining until expiration

Prevailing interest rates

Dividend, if any, paid by the underlying stock

Volatility

Volatility is the most important of these factors, and is the least understood. The short story is: the more volatile a stock, the more its options are worth. You can obtain higher option premium when writing put options on volatile stocks. BUT be warned that option premium is high for a reason and there is always the chance your stock will undergo a severe price decline and leave you with a significant loss. Writing options on much less volatile stocks is less risky, but the rewards are smaller.

TIP: Be comfortable with the possibility of loss when writing put options. Be aware of the volatility of the stocks you choose to trade because volatile stocks will undergo significant price changes from time to time.

Volatility is a vital topic when trading options and is definitely a topic worth your time to understand. However, it is beyond the scope of this short book.

Part II Nuts and Bolts of Writing Put Options

Chapter 9

Let's Make Some Money

When the opportunity presents itself, you must be ready to make the trade. Thus, it is important to find a good entry point for a trade. To do that, you must be prepared (do your homework). Because investors and traders often have different objectives when trading, the list of things to do in preparation for a trade is similar, but not identical for each group. Please read about both investors and traders to ensure that you get the most new ideas out of this book.

Investors

Periodically update a list of stocks that you want to own and prices you are willing to pay.

Know which strike prices exist for each stock on the list and which option(s) you plan to sell — when other considerations are ideal. (For example, you still have a bullish bias on the stock under the market conditions that exist when the put premium is high enough to sell.)

Monitor the market price of those put options under consideration. You don't want to miss your opportunity to make the trade.

If the put price nears your target, enter a limit order, good for the day. Re-enter it each morning until the order is filled or until you change your mind.

Use day orders; never GTC (Good 'til Cancelled) to eliminate all possibility that you will forget than you entered the order. In addition, if the stock gap-opens lower, you do not want to get your order filled at a bad price.

26

Know the option premium necessary to provide an opportunity to buy stock at your price. For example, if the target entry price is $28.80 per share, then you can sell a put option struck at $30 when the premium is $1.20 or higher.

TIP: If you want to pay that $28.80 after commissions, then add the commissions to the desired premium. If it costs $15 to make the trade and you plan to sell three options, then you need an extra $5 per option. That raises the minimum premium $28.85.

NOTE: You are not guaranteed to get the stock. If the put option expires worthless, or if you repurchase that option before expiration, then you cannot be assigned an exercise notice and you will not buy the shares. However, you do get to keep the option premium (minus any cost to repurchase) as your profit for the trade.

If you believe in technical analysis (and even if you don't) be aware of support and resistance levels for your stocks.

TIP: Consider writing a put option when the stock price is slightly above support. Then if the stock price dips and breaks support, you can exit with a small loss. And when support holds, you will have a profitable trade.

For maximum time decay and maximum annualized return, write options expiring in the front month (or week, if Weeklys options are available). Keep in mind that short-term options may come with annualized higher reward potential, but they also come with added risk (more negative gamma).

For maximum protection against loss (when the stock declines too far) sell options with a higher premium. The best way to do that is to sell options with a bit longer lifetime – perhaps 3-6 months. The higher premium provides a lower break-even price for the trade, although it does give more time for things to go wrong. There is always a tradeoff.

Traders

Maintain a list of stocks on which you are short-term bullish.

If *timing the trade* is of primary importance, then choose the most appropriate option to sell at the time you plan to trade. There is no reason to decide which option to sell in advance, because your goal is to make a trading profit and your plan does not include buying the stock.

If *choosing a price level* (presumably near support) is your primary concern, be prepared to write put options when the stock nears that price. Then choose a slightly out-of-the-money put option whose strike price is just below the support level.

If the *premium* is of utmost importance, closely monitor put prices. When the profit potential looks attractive, enter a limit (never a market) sell order.

How to enter a trade as an investor

There are two situations in which you, the investor, want to write naked put options:

- You are willing to buy stock, if necessary, but prefer to earn a trading profit. If that describes you, then write put options that meet your requirements for profit potential (if it expires worthless) both in dollars and in ROI (return on investment). Look for an opportunity to repurchase the option when you are satisfied with the profit.

- You are eager to purchase stock for your portfolio

- o Decide the price you are willing to pay, just as when you enter any order to buy stock.

- o Calculate the option premium required so that you pay that price (or less) when assigned an exercise notice.

- o Calculate the potential profit if the put expires worthless. Is the trade worthwhile, or should you buy stock? Do not sell put options for a very small premium.

Example

a) You have been watching WNP for some time. It is currently trading @ $42 and you want buy 500 shares @ $38.

b) If you write a put option with a $40 strike price, and if the premium is $2 or higher, and if you are eventually assigned an exercise notice, then you will have achieved your goal.

NOTE: If you want to buy the shares at $38 after expenses, then try to collect an extra 5 or 10 cents when selling the put. Just recognize that if you do try for that small amount of extra premium, you may occasionally miss a good trade.

c) Knowing that you require a premium of $2.10 (the extra $0.10 is to pay for trading expenses) to sell the option, find the nearest expiration date that has a sufficient premium.

TIP: Obviously, it is best to sell the near-term put and collect your target premium of $2.10. This may require waiting for the stock price to decline. If you prefer not to wait, it may be worthwhile to write the put two or three months prior to expiration so that you can collect the minimum acceptable premium.

There is no rule of thumb in this scenario. How long you are willing to hold the position in an effort to achieve your goal (buying the stock) is a personal decision. If waiting six months works for you, then sell the 6-month option. Crunch the numbers and when the potential profit over the lifetime of the option meets your needs, then the trade is probably a good one for you.

How to enter a trade as a trader

When writing put options, there are fewer considerations for a trader than for an investor, so be certain not to skip the advice for investors (above) because that discussion encompasses important information – and a way of thinking about writing put options that may be applicable to you, the trader.

When ready to pull the trigger, choose an option with a strike price and expiration date that suits your expectations for the stock.

- Because your goal is to earn a profit, and not to accumulate stock, write out-of-the-money puts.

- If you are exceedingly bullish, this may not be the best strategy because profits are limited. However, you can afford to write a put with a higher strike price and attempt to earn the larger premium.

- If your expectation for the future price of the stock involves a specific time frame, then choose an option that expires within that time. Otherwise shorter-term options (one to four weeks) have relatively rapid time decay, and that is a good thing for the short-term trader.

TIP: Avoid very low priced options. The risk is too great and the potential profit is much too small. Do not overlook how much is at risk when seeking the reward (profit).

TIP: If you trade very short-term (one week) options, be aware that the rewards may come very quickly, but these options are not very far out of the money and provide a relatively small premium, so that a less-than-significant decline in the stock price may be enough to generate a large loss. You will quickly discover which expiration dates are comfortable to trade.

The biggest adjustment for very short-term put sellers is the holding period for the trade. Because options tend to have wide bid/ask spreads, and because you must overcome that bid/ask differential with each trade, short holding periods (less than a day or two) are contraindicated unless the stock makes a quick and significant move higher.

If your trade preference is to be in and out of a trade quickly, you are forced to trade options that expire in one week or less. If that turns out to be uncomfortable, then selling naked puts may not be appropriate. On the other hand, this strategy allows for a very nice profit coupled with a high probability of success when your prognosticating skills are working well.

If 'short-term' for you is 'several weeks' then consider writing options expiring in the front 2 months. A trader (vs. an investor) rarely writes an option with a longer expiration.

You may occasionally want to add stock to your investment portfolio (IRA account, for example). When that happens, write at-the-money puts (or even slightly in-the-money puts). Why the more aggressive strike price? Because — as a trader — you have a short-term bullish bias. If that bias is based on a proven track record, then selling short-term puts should be more effective than short-term swing trading (you gain from time decay in addition to gaining when the stock price behaves).

Calculate the potential profit for each trade and proceed only when satisfied with that return on your investment.

Considerations when entering a trade

Example:

WXY, a reasonably volatile stock, is currently trading @ $30 per share.

Accept the following four statements as true:

1) Either you are an investor interested in buying WXY @ $27 or you are a trader who is interested in opening a bullish position near the current price level.

2) It is Monday, immediately following March expiration (traditional 3rd Friday of the month). April expiration arrives in four weeks and May expiration comes five later.

3) The Apr 30 put is 1.25 bid. The Apr 27 ½ put is 0.55 bid.

4) The May 30 put is 2.00 bid. The May 27 ½ put is 0.95 bid.

Mr. or Ms. Investor:

Sell the Apr 27 ½ put @ $55 per contract.

If the stock remains above the strike price when expiration day arrives, you earn a profit of $55, or approximately 2% ROI (when you have $2,750 in your account; i.e., the put position is cash backed).

If the stock is below the strike price on expiration day, you will be assigned an exercise notice, and buy the stock @ $26.95 per share ($27.50 less the 0.55 received earlier). This is the price you wanted to pay to own this stock.

Either result is good.

Mr. or Ms. Trader:

Sell either the Apr 30 put or the Apr 27 ½ put. Selling either put gives you the opportunity to earn a decent profit when the stock performs as predicted (you are bullish).

Choose the Apr 30 put if confident that the stock is going higher. You can earn up to $125 per option, when the option eventually expires worthless. This entails a higher probability of losing money than selling the lower struck put, but the potential reward (4.3% return; $125/$2875) makes this play tempting for the bullish trader.

Choose the safer (loses money less often) Apr 27 ½ put if you are only mildly bullish. The profit potential is only $55 (2% return), but your chances of earning that profit are higher.

You can sell either of the May puts if you prefer additional insurance (lower break-even price) at the cost of a reduced annualized return. Most short-term traders reject this choice because of the longer holding period, but anyone concerned about preservation of capital and minimizing risk should seriously consider writing a later-dated option.

NEGATIVES when selling puts: From the point of view as a trader, the profit potential is limited. If you buy the stock, it is possible to earn a much more substantial profit.

POSITIVES when selling puts: You can earn a profit when the stock price does not rise. If you write the put, time becomes your ally, especially when the stock price remains relatively unchanged. If you choose the lower strike price (an out-of-the-money put) you earn money even if the stock price declines. That's a new experience for a bullish trader and should more than compensate for limiting your profit potential.

TIP: As a trader, there is no reason to hold the position until expiration. Close the position (by buying back the put that you sold) any time you are satisfied with the profit, you are no longer bullish on the stock, or the option price becomes so low that there is no point it taking the risk to earn an extra $5 or $10 on the option).

Exiting a trade

Knowing when to exit a trade is often as crucial as knowing when to enter a trade, but it is something often overlooked by option teachers. With this specific strategy knowing when to take your profit and exit is sufficiently important that it should not be overlooked.

Investors seldom close a position before expiration because being assigned an exercise notice is a satisfactory alternative to taking the short-term profit.

Traders must close their profitable positions more often. The decision should be based on the trader's outlook for the stock in the immediate future as well as the time premium remaining in the option. When the potential profit is minimal (because the option can be bought for a very low premium) prudence dictates taking the profit and moving on to the next trade. I agree that it may seem foolish to pay $0.05 to cover a short position that appears to be 'very safe' to hold. However, 'very safe' is not good enough when the reward is so small. Unexpected events do happen and there is no point in risking several hundred (or thousand) dollars to earn an extra $5.

Chapter 10
Summary: Thought Process When Entering a Trade

When considering whether or not a specific set of conditions is suitable for writing a naked put option, each individual must make a decision. The material in this section offers insight on how you can make a good (for you and your investment approach) decision more frequently.

NOTE: In the following discussion, I describe several different ideas that constitute a way of thinking (mindset) that is rarely, if ever, discussed in options-education material. I believe that considering the ideas mentioned below leads to making a trade more successful.

Example:
Stock UVW is trading @ $41.

It is shortly after the July expiration.

The UVW Aug 40 put can be sold for $1.00.

1) Possible thought process for the investor who is a *first time seller* of a naked put option:

"I'd like to own 400 shares of UVW stock. I'm a bit nervous about selling put options because my full-service broker doesn't think it is a good idea. But this eBook has me convinced that the strategy is more conservative (and profitable) than my broker believes it to be.

"If I go ahead and sell this put option, it is going to be a nervous four weeks as I wait for expiration. But, when I remember that only two things can happen, and each of these possibilities appeals to me, the proposition becomes less

35

frightening. In four weeks I'll either own the 400 shares at $39 per share, or I will have earned $400.

"Of course, I could simply bid $39 for the stock, and there is a chance I'll buy it. But if the stock rallies, as I believe it will, I won't be able to get the stock at my price. If I sell the put option, at least I'll have $400 as a consolation prize if I'm correct in my expectations this stock.

"Okay. I'm going to make this trade tomorrow morning!"

2) Possible thought process for the *experienced* put-selling investor:

"I've been watching UVW and it is been approaching my target buy price of $39. I'm going to write the Aug 40 puts for a buck ($1.00). In any event, I'm a winner. I'll either own 400 shares at $39, or I'll keep the premium and walk away with $400."

3) Possible thought process for the trader making his *first trade* using put options:

"UVW is $41 and approaching support at $40.50. I'm convinced that taking a long position in the stock is the right move. I believe the stock price will increase within several months. Of course, I can simply buy stock, but if I understand correctly, there are advantages to selling the put option. I know my profit is limited to only $100 per put (the premium), but in return for limiting the possible profit, my break-even point drops from the current price of $41 to $39. I'd like that extra safety cushion.

"Because my work does not predict an immediate price increase, by selling the put option I will get paid to have patience. If I buy stock now, I'll have to pay cash. If UVW remains locked in a narrow range near its support level, I would gain nothing. But, if I sell naked puts, I not only collect the option premium, but I'll keep my cash and earn interest on it.

"Yes, put selling seems like a good idea in this scenario and I'm going to jump into this strategy first thing tomorrow morning. I may even try to make a bit extra and attempt to sell the put for $1.05."

4) Possible thought process for the *experienced* put-writing trader:

"The UVW chart looks good here, but the stock may stay in a trading range before breaking out to the upside. I've seen this too many times before. Instead of buying stock, I'll write these August 40 puts for $1. Sure, it limits profits, but I want to make some money just in case the stock trades in a narrow range for a while.

"If the stock doesn't move much in a month, I'll probably want to sell the September 40 puts, but I may elect to buy the stock. For now, I'm writing Aug 40 puts and giving up the chance to make a larger profit in return for a better chance to earn any profit."

Mark D Wolfinger

Look on ShareScope and
pick out shares in
either up or downtrends
by looking at the
"Tram Lines"

Chapter 11
What Can Go Wrong?

As with any stock market investment, investors with if a long (bullish) position runs the risk of a declining stock market during which their specific investment loses value. Writing put options is very similar to owning stock when the market declines and you should expect to lose money when adopting this method during bear markets. However, the difference between the seller of naked puts and the stockholder is that the former has some protection against loss –the premium collected when selling the puts.

What choices do you have if the stock moves against you (lower)?

Repair Strategies: What to do if a position goes awry.

Assume you decided to write the WXY Apr 27 ½ put @ $0.55.

Scenario: Assume WXY rapidly declines to $24 per share.

There are several reasonable choices, depending on your priorities:

- If you are content to own the stock at $26.95, with the risk of losing money when the stock declines further, then do nothing. No repair is necessary.

- Most traders believe it is good money management to minimize losses, and I urge you to do so. If you want to cut losses now, then buy WXY Apr 27 ½ puts to close the position. It is sometimes necessary to take a loss on a trade and accept the fact that not every trade can be profitable.

- If you want to maintain a long position in WXY, then one idea is to <u>roll the position</u> by buying the Apr 27 ½ put sold earlier and simultaneously (or immediately thereafter) selling a new put option with a lower strike price and/or a more distant expiration date. NOTE: Two options are traded at the same time by using a spread order.

Example: Buy Apr 27 ½ put (to close your current position) and sell Jul 25 (or perhaps Oct 25 or Oct 22 ½) put to open a new position.

Having decided roll and continue to own a long position in WXY, there are two choices to consider: Decide which of the following is more important for you. (There is no correct choice that suites every trader.)

- Gain protection against a further decline. Minimize the potential loss. This is my choice.

- Give yourself the best chance to turn this position profitable as time passes. This involves greater downside risk, but is suitable if you *still have a bullish outlook on WXY*.

TIP: It is mandatory for your future success as an option trader to understand this important idea:

> **Do not stubbornly refuse to take a loss.**

Translation: Never hold a position because closing it would lock in a loss. You already earned the loss, and hoping for things to turn around is not an acceptable strategy. However, if you still want to own the position – as an independent decision – then repairing (adjusting) the position to something that is currently suitable makes sense.

Example:

Two weeks pass and WXY declined to $24.

Accept the following four statements as true:

1) Apr 27 ½ put is offered @ $4

2) Jul 25 put is $2.25 bid

3) Oct 22 ½ put is $2.00 bid

4) Oct 25 put is $3.10 bid

What should you do? There is no 'right' choice when rolling a position. It is reasonable to buy the April put and sell any of the 3 puts listed. It is also reasonable to pay $4 to cover the Apr 27½ put that you are short and abandon the trade.

TIP: Choose the option that fits your 'comfort' zone. Be certain you want to own the new position (BEFORE owning it) and don't force the trade 'just to do something'. If you don't know which position you want to own, close the position and accept the loss

If you are more concerned with protection (reducing the likelihood of incurring additional losses), then write the farther out-of-the-money Oct 22 ½ put.

NEGATIVES: You will own a position with more than five months until expiration.

POSITIVES: The Oct 22 ½ put is out of the money and has a reasonable chance to expire worthless. This allows for the possibility of earning enough money to offset a substantial portion of the current loss.

Let's look at the numbers:

When October expiration arrives:

- If WXY is higher than $22.50, the put expires worthless. You collected $55 for the initial sale, paid $400 to repurchase the put, and collected $200 for selling the Oct put. All in all, you paid $145 for the position, you have no remaining position, and $145 is the loss.

- That loss is not too bad, considering you went long WXY when it was near $30 and watched it drop to $24. You cut immediate risk of additional losses by rolling and maintaining a position. If you had paid $4 to cover the Apr put, the loss would have been $345 per option ($400 minus $55).

- If WXY is below $22.50, you will be assigned an exercise notice. The shares cost $22.50 (strike) less the premium collected (-$1.45) for selling the put. In this example, you 'collected' a negative amount and your shares cost $23.95 each. This is considerably better than the $26.95 it would have cost if you simply held and did not roll the position.

You now own the shares (when assigned on the Oct 22 ½ put). What should you do next? This topic is covered below.

If you are still bullish and want to own a position in WXY, then sell the Oct 25 put @ $3.10. It will cost $90 to roll the position (pay $400 for Apr, collect $310 for Oct). Because you collected $55 for the initial sale, you now have now incurred a debit of $35 cash (plus commissions).

NOTE: Do not make this play in an attempt to 'recover your lost money.' It is no longer your money because it belongs to someone else. Only make this trade if you truly – as an independent decision – want to be naked short the WXY Oct 25 puts when the stock is $24.

When October expiration arrives

- If WXY is above $25, the put expires worthless and your loss is only $35. That's an excellent result, considering how far WXY moved against you.

- If WXY is below $25 you will be assigned an exercise notice and pay $25 for the stock, making your true cost $25.35 per share.

- Because the stock is trading @ $24 at the time you rolled the position, it is reasonable to expect to be assigned that exercise notice when expiration day arrives. See the next section for what to do next

What to do if you are assigned an exercise notice at expiration:

If the put is in the money at expiration, you can expect to be assigned an exercise notice and own a long position in the stock. Of course, if you are an investor, you can simply keep the stock and hope for the best. But, there is a better strategy.

TIP: Now that you own stock, you can sell someone else the right to buy that stock. You do that by selling a call option and collecting a cash premium.

This idea should feel familiar to you, because you made a very similar trade when writing a naked put option: You sold someone else the right to sell stock to you at the strike price for a limited amount of time. The mechanics are exactly the same when you sell a call option, and the strategy is called covered call writing: You sell someone else the right to buy your stock at the strike price for a limited amount of time. And you collect the option premium.

In our examples above, October expiration just passed and you own WXY stock (@ 23.95 in the first scenario or @ 25.35 in the second scenario. You can write the Nov 25 call or the Dec 25 call, collect a premium and give yourself an excellent chance to earn enough to make the whole trade (including the original sale of the put option) profitable.

The discussion of covered call writing requires a separate book of its own.

Chapter 12

What to do when Expiration Day Arrives

Expiration day is nothing to fear. In fact, most of the time it represents another opportunity to make money.

a) If the puts that you sold are out of the money, and you have not yet covered the short position, do nothing. Allow them to expire worthless. Once expiration is past and you have not been assigned an exercise notice, all obligations have been removed and the following Monday (when the market opens again) you can reinvest the capital that was tied up as collateral for your recently expired positions. Translation: You may decide to sell new put options.

NOTE: Although options cease trading when the market closes on expiration Friday, the official expiration day is the next day, or Saturday. You will not know whether you were assigned an exercise notice or whether the options expired worthless until notified by your broker. That notification is available Sunday – if you have access to your account via the Internet. However, the brokers are required to let you know no later than the following Monday morning, before the market opens for trading. The best thing you can do to avoid mistakes is to examine your portfolio early Monday. If you bought the shares (via being assigned) you will see the shares in your account (and cash to pay for them 'missing.' If the options expired worthless, then the shares will not be in your account.

TIP: By waiting until Monday to write new puts on the same stock, you run some risk. If the stock opens higher the puts will be priced lower than they were last Friday. Of course, the stock may open lower and you would be able to collect a higher premium than you anticipated.

45

If the put you plan to sell next Monday is attractively priced on expiration Friday, consider buying back the worthless put for $0.05 and selling the attractively priced put. Understand that it is not necessary to wait until expiration Friday to make this play. Any time the put you are short can be bought cheaply and the put you want to write is attractively priced, it is reasonable to make this switch (exit current put and substitute another) rather than wait for expiration to arrive.

NOTE: It is generally a poor idea to tell yourself that an option sold earlier is 'so far out of the money' there is no risk it will ever go into the money. It may be tempting to ignore these out of the money puts and simply sell new puts on the same stock, but I urge you not to do so. If an unexpected disaster strikes, your position would be twice the size you want it to be. This can be a dangerous situation, resulting in a large loss. Don't be greedy for that extra $0.05 per contract. Do not sell new puts until the current puts have been covered. Even if it is late in the afternoon on expiration Friday, be careful, because stocks have been known to gap lower at the end of a trading day.

NOTE: If you are fully invested and have no remaining buying power in your account, you cannot write new puts until the old puts have expired or have been repurchased (covered).

TIP: If you maintain a up-to-date list of potential investment opportunities, the weekend after expiration is the ideal time to select your top candidates in preparation for trading next Monday morning. The Monday after expiration is a good time to write new puts and begin putting your cash to work for the following month.

b) If the expiring puts are in the money, you have three reasonable alternatives:

- Cover. You have a profit or loss depending on how the price you paid to cover compares with the original premium collected.

- Allow yourself to be assigned an exercise notice. You will own a long position in the underlying stock. You can write covered call options, if that appeals to you.

- Roll the position. Buy back the put sold earlier and write a put option expiring in a future month. In the repair strategy described earlier, you rolled a position in order to reduce risk. In this scenario, the position can be rolled to seek additional profits.

TIP: Never roll the position just to have something to do. If you are not satisfied with the option prices available, then cover the short put or allow yourself to be assigned. Forcing a trade is a very poor strategy. You want to roll the position only when the profit potential is satisfactory. It is not essential to own a position in this stock at this time. Own a position when both the profit potential and risk are favorable, and not otherwise.

Mark D Wolfinger

Chapter 13
Conclusion

Writing naked puts is a strategy suitable for most investors, even though many investment professionals consider it to be a risky proposition. It is more conservative than simply owning stocks – and almost all professionals consider that strategy to be prudent. Consider it to your advantage that more advisors shun this strategy, because it creates less competition when you want to write your put options. This strategy is used by an ever-increasing number of mutual funds and hedge funds.

One of the great advantages of writing naked put options — and it is for bullish investors and traders — is that you are much more likely to show a profit than when you adopt a strategy of buying and holding stock. When you own stock, its price must increase to generate profits. When writing naked puts, you show a profit if the stock price rises, holds steady, and sometimes even when the stock price declines. Even though your potential profit is limited, the fact that you have so many more winning trades is enough to more than compensate for limited gains.

One word of caution: Naked put writing is a bullish strategy and does not do well in bear markets. Don't sell too many puts at any one time – remember, if you are assigned an exercise notice, you will be buying 100 shares of stock for each put sold.

Happy put writing!

Glossary

At the Money – The strike price of the option is equal (or nearly so) to the price of the underlying stock

Assigned an Exercise Notice – Being notified that the owner of the option contract has exercised his rights, making the recipient obligated to fulfill the conditions of the contract (buy 100 shares of stock at the strike price, if the option sold is a put; sell 100 shares when the option is a call)

Call Option – A contract giving its owner the right to buy a specific item (100 shares of stock) at a specific price (strike price) for a specified period of time (until expiration)

Cash Backed Naked Put – Writing a put option in an account that contains sufficient cash to buy the stock, if the put seller is assigned an exercise notice

Covered Call – A position consisting of short call options and a corresponding long position in the underlying stock of at least 100 shares per call

Expiration – The last date on which the option owner may exercise the option. Once this date comes and goes the unexercised option has lost all value. Although we tend to refer to 'expiration Friday' the true expiration date is the next day, or Saturday.

Expire Worthless – The situation occurs when the option is out of the money at the close of business on expiration Friday and the option owner elects not to exercise

In the Money – An option with an intrinsic value. A put option with a strike price higher than the price of the underlying stock is ITM; a call option with a strike price lower than the price of the underlying stock is ITM

Intrinsic value – The difference between the strike price and the stock price for an ITM option. Example: a put option struck at $25 has an intrinsic value of $1.25 per share, when the stock price is $23.75.

Leg – As a noun, it is one part of a spread position. As a verb it means to place a trade, intending to eventually enter another trade to complete a spread.

Leverage – The degree to which an investor is using borrowed money. Reward potential is high, but risk is even higher because the investor can lose not only his own money, but borrowed funds as well.

Margin – The deposit made to a brokerage account in the form of cash or eligible securities; collateral to protect the broker against loss

Margin Call – The demand for additional collateral to be deposited to a brokerage account; If funds are not deposited immediately, the broker has the right to close any position(s) deemed necessary to protect the firm against loss.

Obligations – The required actions of an option seller who has been assigned an exercise notice. With puts, the person assigned is obligated to purchase 100 shares (per put option) at the strike price. When the option is a call, the person must sell 100 shares at the strike price. Once assigned, the ensuing trade cannot be broken.

Out of the Money – A situation in which the option has no intrinsic value. A put option with a strike price lower than the underlying stock price or a call option with a strike price higher than the stock price

Premium – The price the buyer pays, and the seller receives, when an option trade occurs

Put option – A contract giving its owner the right to sell a specific item (100 shares of stock) at a specific price (strike price) for a specified period of time (until expiration)

Resistance —The price that a stock has previously shown an inability to penetrate to the upside

Roll a Position – Buy to cover a previously sold option and simultaneously (by entering a spread order) sell another option. That new option is often farther out of the money with a longer-dated expiration

Spread Order – An order to buy one option and sell another. The broker is obligated to complete both the buy and sell. The trader who entered the order gets both options or none. There is no risk of filling only one side of the order.

Spread Position – A hedged (risk-reducing) position consisting of two or more different options on different sides of the market (i.e., one option represents a bullish position on the stock and the other represents a bearish position on the stock)

Strike price – The price at which the owner of an option contract has the right to buy (call) or sell (put) the underlying

Struck at $30 – The option strike price is $30

Support – A price that a stock has previously shown an inability to penetrate to the downside

Synthetic Put – A position that behaves exactly the same as a put option, but is not a put option. The covered call position (long 100 shares; short one call) is a synthetic put

Uncovered (Naked) – An option position that does not have an offsetting position in the underlying stock. For the sale of a put option to be 'covered' the account must own a different put option or be short at least 100 shares of the underlying stock. The recommended strategy (writing naked puts) contains no such offsetting position, and the put is uncovered

Underlying – The stock from which the option derives its value. It is the item an option owner has the right to buy (call) or sell (put)

Volatility – A measure of the tendency of a stock to undergo price changes. It is also the tendency of the option premium to change. The options on highly volatile stocks are expensive and are very sensitive to the stock price. Options on low volatility stocks are less expensive and are less sensitive to a change in the stock price.

Appendix: An Introduction to Equivalent Positions

July 27, 2008 blog post

One of the interesting features about options is that there is a relationship between calls, puts, and the underlying stock. And because of that relationship, some option positions are equivalent to others– that means they have identical profit/loss profiles.

Why is that important? You will discover that some option combinations – called spreads – are easier, or less costly to trade than others. Even with today's low commissions, why spend more than you must?

The basic (simplified to ignore the cost of owning stock) equation that describes an underlying and its options is: Owning one call option and selling one put option (with the same strike price and expiration date) is equivalent to owning 100 shares of stock. Thus,

$S = C - P$; where S = stock; C = call; P = put

If you want a simple proof that the above equation is true, consider a position that is long one call and short one put. When expiration arrives, if the call option is in the money, you exercise the call and own 100 shares. If the put option is in the money, you are assigned an exercise notice and buy 100 shares of stock. In either case, you own stock. NOTE: If the stock is at the money when expiration arrives, you are in a quandary. You don't know if the put owner is going to exercise and therefore, you don't know whether to exercise the call. If you want to maintain the long stock position, the simplest way out is to buy the put, paying $0.05, or less, and exercising the call.

There is one equivalent position that you, the put seller, should know because these are strategies you are likely to adopt.

Take a look at a covered call position (long stock and short one call), or S-C.

From the equation above, $S - C = -P$. In other words, if you own stock and sell one call option (covered call) then your position is equivalent to being short one put option with the same strike and expiration. That position is naked short the put. Amazingly some brokers don't allow all clients to sell naked puts, but they allow all to write covered calls. The world is not always logical (you already knew that).

Thus, writing a covered call is equivalent to selling a naked put. This is not a big deal to anyone who is an experienced option trader, but to a newcomer to the world of options this can be an eye-opener.

The more you trade options, you more you will become aware of other equivalent positions. You may even decide to play with the equation yourself and discover others.

###

Mark D Wolfinger

Thank you for buying Writing Naked Puts

Join my e-mail list for occasional updates:

Visit my blog:

    For 1,000 great articles about trading options.

    Special promotions and discounts.

    Information on new books.

Ask questions: rookies (at) mdwoptions (dot) com

Other Books by Mark D Wolfinger

My Dead-Tree Books
The Rookies Guide to Options, 2nd Edition (2013)
Create your own Hedge Fund (2005)
The Short Book on Options (2002)

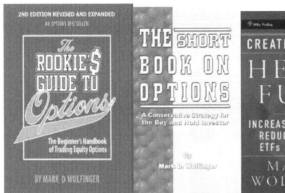

The Best Option Strategies Series of eBooks
Book One. (Volume 0) Intro to Options: The Basics (2014).
Book Two. (Volume 1) Writing Naked Puts (2014).
Book Three (Volume 2) Iron Condors (2014).

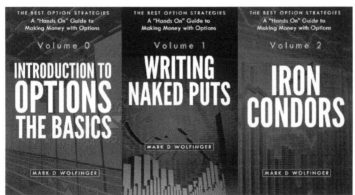

Mark D Wolfinger

My other eBooks:

The Short Book on Options (2002, 2014)
The Option Trader's Mindset: Think like a Winner (2012)
Lessons of a Lifetime: My 33 years as an Option Trader
(2010)

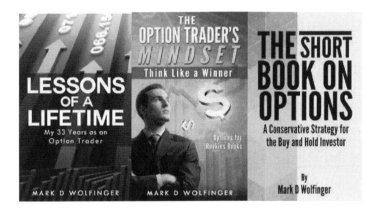

Available at your favorite bookseller

About the Author

Mark Wolfinger has been in the options business since 1977, starting as a market maker on the trading floor of the Chicago Board Options Exchange. He is now an author and educator of individual investors, specializing in the conservative use stock options.

Born in Brooklyn, New York in 1942, he resides in Evanston, Illinois with his life partner Penny.

He received a BS degree from Brooklyn College and a PhD from Northwestern University (Chemistry).

His blog: http://blog.mdwoptions.com
He writes on options for about.com:
http://options.about.com

59

Printed in Great Britain
by Amazon